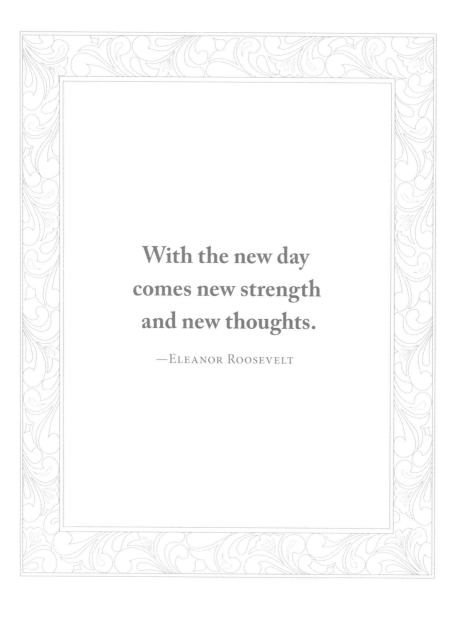

With the new day comes new strength and new thoughts.

—ELEANOR ROOSEVELT

Every day is a new beginning. Treat it that way. Stay away from what might have been, and look at what can be.

—MARSHA PETRIE SUE

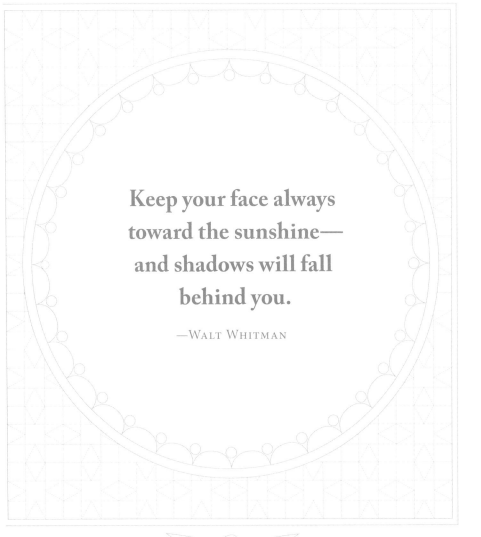

Keep your face always
toward the sunshine—
and shadows will fall
behind you.

—Walt Whitman

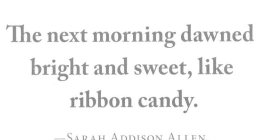

The next morning dawned
bright and sweet, like
ribbon candy.

—Sarah Addison Allen,
Garden Spells

With this morning's
sunrise comes a day
of things that have
never been.

—TONI SORENSON

I arise full of eagerness
and energy, knowing
well what achievement
lies ahead of me.

—Zane Grey

No matter how
gloomy the morning,
it is a new day where
anything is possible.

—JEFFREY FRY

Every sunset is an
opportunity to reset.
Every sunrise begins
with new eyes.

—Richie Norton

Every mountaintop is
within reach if you just
keep climbing.

—Barry Finlay,
Kilimanjaro and Beyond

I hope you realize that every day is a fresh start for you. That every sunrise is a new chapter in your life waiting to be written.

—JUANSEN DIZON,
CONFESSIONS OF A WALLFLOWER

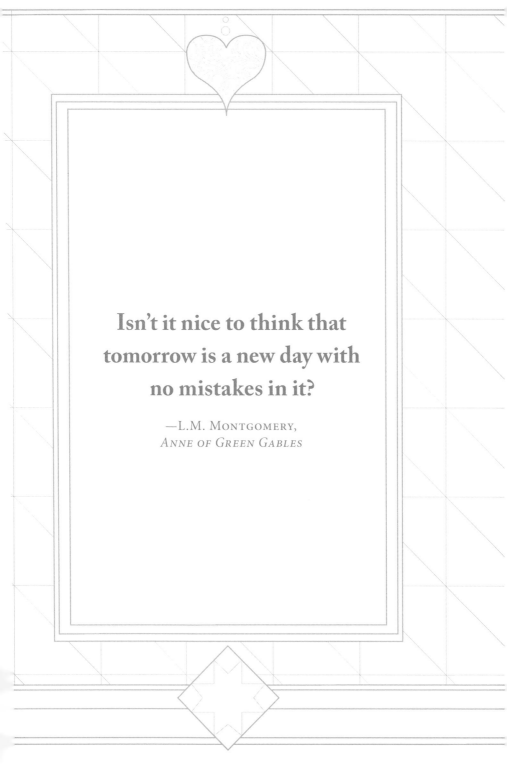

Isn't it nice to think that tomorrow is a new day with no mistakes in it?

—L.M. MONTGOMERY,
ANNE OF GREEN GABLES

Each day provides its
own gifts.

—Marcus Aurelius

About Jim Shore

Jim Shore grew up in rural South Carolina, the son of artistic parents who instilled a love of American folk art. His grandmother was a master quilter who taught him the patience and skill to bring intricate designs to life. Jim worked for decades developing his craft, manufacturing his own designs, and traveling the country to sell his work. Finally, in 2001, he partnered with Enesco to create Heartwood Creek, the successful brand that brought Jim worldwide fame. Jim has received multiple awards from prestigious trade organizations, including the ICON HONORS Life Accomplishment Award in 2012. Through his partnership with Enesco, the Jim Shore Collection has grown from a small group of Santas, snowmen, and angels to a broad year-round brand respected and sold around the world. Jim's boundless creativity and unique ability enable him to touch people in all walks of life through his art.

ISBN 978-1-64178-114-5

Fox Chapel Publishing makes every effort to use environmentally friendly paper for printing.

We are always looking for talented authors and artists. To submit an idea, please send a brief inquiry to acquisitions@foxchapelpublishing.com.

Printed in Singapore
First printing